W9-AAC-240

Sports Biographies

Marion Jones
World-Class Runner

Heather Feldman

Rigby.

Marion Jones: World-Class Runner
Copyright © 2001 by Rosen Book Works, Inc.

On Deck® Reading Libraries
Published by Rigby
1000 Hart Road
Barrington, IL 60010-2627
www.rigby.com

Book Design: Michael de Guzman
Text: Heather Feldman
Photo Credits: Cover © Mike Powell/AllSport; pp. 5, 19 © Clive
Mason/AllSport; p. 7 © Mike Powell/AllSport; p. 9 © Rob Tringali
Jr./SportsChrome; pp. 11, 15 © Bongarts Photography/SportsChrome;
p.13 © Doug Pensinger/AllSport; pp. 17, 21 © Gary M. Prior/AllSport.

All rights reserved. No part of this publication may be reproduced
or transmitted in any form or by any means, electronic or mechanical,
including photocopying, recording, taping, or any information storage
and retrieval system, without permission in writing from the publisher.

On Deck® is a trademark of Reed Elsevier Inc. registered
in the United States and/or other jurisdictions

06 05 04
10 9 8 7 6 5 4 3

Printed in China

ISBN 0-7635-7842-8

Contents

Meet Marion Jones

Marion Jones is a runner.
Marion runs fast.

Working Hard

Marion works hard at being
a fast runner.

Marion works out to stay in shape. Staying in shape helps Marion run fast.

A Great Athlete

Marion is also a great jumper.
Marion jumps high.

Marion played basketball, too. She played basketball in college. Marion is a great athlete.

Winning Races

Marion gets a medal when she wins a race. She kisses the medal. Marion is happy when she runs well.

Marion gets flowers when she wins a race. Marion wins a lot of races. Marion is one of the best runners in the world.

Marion has a lot of fans. She waves to her fans.

Marion runs for the United States. She wins medals for the United States. She likes to win. Most of all, Marion likes to run!

Glossary

athlete (**ath**-leet) someone trained in sports

jumper (**juhm**-puhr) someone who jumps

Resources

Books

Marion Jones: Sprinting Sensation
by Mark Stewart
Children's Press (2000)

Marion Jones: The Fastest Woman
by Bill Gutman
Pocket Books (2000)

Web Site

http://www.waycoolrunning.com

Care was taken in selecting Internet sites. However, Internet addresses can change, or sites can be under construction or no longer exist.

Rigby is not responsible for the content of any Web site listed in this book except its own. All material contained on these sites is the responsibility of its hosts and creators.

Index